Forgotten iPhone Notes That Deserve To Be Remembered

Moná Thomas

BookLeaf Publishing
India | USA | UK

Presentation by *BookLeaf Publishing*

Web: www.bookleafpub.com

E-mail: info@bookleafpub.com

ISBN: 9789357215589

First edition 2022

Dedicated to Jackie Goneze and all of her inspirational meddling.

Bohemia

Today I decided to work in a new cafe,
which turned out to be a community center,
and also an art gallery of the local artists' work.
In a section of Brooklyn that smelled like
rebellion
covered in stickers indie bands.
I felt odd.

I walked in cautiously, but proudly, and looked
around at the messy of it all.
Plastic chairs around wooden tables,
a coffee table next to a burgundy love seat in the
corner,
and a tattered green-patterned chair that was
definitely fetched from the sidewalk.
Windows covered with ads and posters and
reminders
and protests colliding with the colorful art work
covering the walls,
protruding towards the tabletops and floors with
sculptures
and funky lamps with more dangling art that
resembled handmade jewelry made with stones,
seeds, beads, and puka shells.
Indescribable claustrophobia settled in.

I read the menu—printed on yellow sheets of paper hanging from the counter by a string of yarn—over and over, for no real reason outside of catching my breathe. Until I look up and just order a coffee from the white guy with a long scruff beard, the facial hair being held together with multiple rubber bands creating a face sword, and a sandwich from the guy who looks like Elton John and speaks with a smile.

I grabbed my coffee and walked slowly to the green chair and sunk into its cushioned abyss of a seat. Elton brought me my order and I sipped from my coffee. It was terrible. I bit my sandwich. It tasted plain and homemade. I loved it.

Nostalgia washes over me. And I conclude, younger me would have made this place home. In all of its mess, it felt cluttered and 23-year-old me would have rolled around in its complicated art statements and open mic night snaps like memory foam. I laugh out loud, to myself.

How funny is it to realize that I've been attracted to communities my entire life, and they find me, when I'm not paying attention.

note to self

if ever you are curious about how well you're doing in life, just remember you created the goals in your mind. you can choose what it looks like to win.

—

i like how “i write poems about you” and “i talk to my therapist about you” are both a compliment and an insult depending on intent because they both require a deep, intense, and intentional connection to our emotions. whatever they may be.

my mother didn't believe in art therapy

and she asked the doctor,
"and what am i supposed to do
when she just goes home
and draws flowers?"

Levé

when i moved to atlanta in 2017, i lost my entire library of books and notebooks. i still catch myself in conversations mentioning a book i have or a poem i wrote, forgetting that those things don't exist with me anymore. it's heartbreaking. of all the books i've bought, was gifted, stood in lines for, or found, i don't miss any one of them more than this—the one i found underneath a bookshelf in a housing works, thrifting with friends on a day i wasn't even supposed to be with them. it was a random buy, but i have a thing about buying galley copies if i find them. in thrift stores or on the streets. it feels like housing unwanted, forgotten children. there aren't many books that cross my mind or heart regularly, but this is one of them. it found me at a time when i was attempting to write a manuscript in a style i've never seen before and wasn't sure it was going to work. spirit sent me the example. i didn't remember buying this copy and i came home tonight to it—after having the realization on the subway that i'm in a phase of moving on and moving forward with all of my inner parts. and it's almost comical because i ordered a new copy without thinking, but now i understand the message that was moving through me: my copy, with all of my notes and highlights and underlines and circles, is gone, but the book still exists. and i can now create new memories with an old friend and maybe find something new in between its lines. if not, it's still a beautiful piece of literature.

are you rising?

do you know how lucky you are?
to be with a woman so grounded in her divine femininity
that she remains unshaken by your masculine?
so firm in her womanhood that she, in all of her glory,
chose you? how lucky you must feel,
to be chosen by a woman.
holding a hand with her intuition while venting to the moon. what privilege
you have
to be loved by a woman.
cared for by a woman.
given permission to have space by an entity so mystical,
she is still learning herself
and grows more powerful with each lesson.
and, miraculously, still has energy to give to you
and your journey
and your mission
and your truth. so much so, that she is not dwindled by your path,
but empowered to be able to instill power into another spirit she comes across.
do you see it?

or have you squandered such an opportunity to rise, to such an occasion?

i purchased my first mattress at the age of 26.

this tuft and needle is more than
a stack of materials
built for my physical comfort.
it is stability.
it is welcome home.
it is ownership.
it is security.
it is a checkpoint in the race i felt like
i kept getting tripped in.
it is the tuft of peace growing around me
that i wasn't able to see.
it is the needle popping the unrealistic
expectations
of me not making it.
it is love.
it is meditation space.
it is office.
it is opportunity knocking on my pillows.
it is sanctuary.
it is confessional.
it is lover's space.
it is made for the king in my queen silhouette.
it is mine.
it is mine.
it is, mine.

—

i will no longer be anyone’s goodie bag of
emotions for them dig their darkened fingers
into when they wish to feel, anything.

commune

my friends spellcheck my spells,
perform my handwritten rituals,
light candles for me and i for them in times of
hardship. we pray and meditate together, suggest
self care practices based on knowledge of each
other's regular routines, check in with each other
when cosmic phenomenons are occurring and
someone doesn't know what's going on.
we drop knowledge on each other in our given
crafts, we fact check one another,
drop book titles, affirmations, planetary shifts,
and songs that stir the soul in the group chat.
we share fears and doubts and crycrycry to each
other when our shells crack.
when this matrix is loud, i cover her ears.
when i drop the ball, he helps me pick it up and
carries it with me.
when she needs time of silence, we drop a veil
over her world and block out all distractions.
a team. a collective consciousness. a family. a
tribe.

my heart burns from the sun
it's being forced to grow.

excuse me while i learn how to breathe fire.

tides of moon

last night i stood in the rain
and felt exhaustion fall from my body.
there is something about water
that has always cleansed my soul.

—

words become heavier as we age.
like stones being laid for a solid path.
our words are what we stand on.

i could have loved you

when i looked into your eyes i saw

and i would have thought i was crazy
until that when you casually told me
i would be with you forever

for some reason right now it wasn't meant to be
and that's okay
because i learned

the summer of retrograde didn't want me to win
but also

so maybe we'll meet again
maybe sooner
maybe later
hell, maybe never

but if we do
but i'm able to look at you
and tell you i love you

this gap in our timeline
would have been worth it.

unconnected lines

i get home sick for people, sometimes.

—

please replenish the wells you drink from.

—

my heart is bloodshot from staying up late,
waiting for you.

the loft

sat in a sex club and talked about classical poetry with the owner. he has a poe portrait which i was intrigued to learn more about. it lead to a conversation about today's poetry, fitness, growth, and folks not understanding the true power of wordsmiths. at the end he told me i give him hope about my generation. i was honored.

pause here

when was the last time
you acknowledged
your own existence?
...

—

i am currently loving from a space where i am swimming in my own feminine divinity. the intimacy i have for other souls have pronounced themselves primarily in masculine vessels. my divine feminine is blossoming into her own essence and has been attracting pure divine masculinity. my space has been an enlightening balance of woman and man. goddess and god. venus and mars. for years i have developed my internal divine masculine and trained that energy to wield such power with regal presence. in this current portal, i am woman. i am she. i am the goddess that has peacefully enjoyed her slumber. i am feminine divine personified. she is awakened, and ready to rule.

the truths

33: be the student.
32: do the work.
31: do it scared.
30: show your work.
29: feel like home.

—

i am so full of joy. there are brief moments in life where the internal universe is silent and i get a chance to put things into perspective a bit. really soak in this time. i am happy, and this isn't something i have owned for long stretches of this life. maybe bursts, but i never actually appreciate bursts neither. so right now, as of late, i sit in my gratitude and in my appreciation for the blessings that i am constantly receiving. it brings to me to tears some days still to think how quickly a situation at my current job was fixed simply and almost entirely on faith. i start a new position this coming monday that i'm genuinely excited to start. i've been holding hands with the concept of freelancing my words for a minute now and now i have three secured clients. i have this inspiring apartment that i fall in love with everyday when i cross its threshold. i have a beautiful man by my side. i have a beautiful woman by my side. i recently discovered an added section to this lifetime's purpose and it has refueled my mission and creativity. my poetic tongue has returned, and i'm in this current moment of trying not to fan girl out when poets and writers i've been lowkey stalking on social media dm me like let's collab or tell me they love the new words i'm putting out and can't wait to see more. my tribe is consistent and supportive and know i am still figuring this shit out and man, the difference there is when there are people who are genuinely in your corner simply off the fact that they fuck with you. it's beautiful and overwhelming sometimes bc some of these homies have seen my struggle through so many personal situations, demons, career setbacks, and lagging creativity or motivation but still on some "you good, you got it" type shit. i don't say any of this to boast or brag or make it seem like i'm entirely elevated. nah, i'm just having a moment of yo, you are truly blessed and as much as i thank source (god/God/universe/allah/jesus/buddha/whatever you connect with) on a daily, i can always do more, i can always act more and be more intentional with these practices. i fast on monday's for shiva, i recite mantras daily for parvati, i laugh joyously for ganesh. i live for this mission, perpetually adjusting to living my truths and truths that are still being discovered. i am thankful and appreciative for being chosen for such an important path in this timeline. i am truly blessed and constantly thinking, what more can i do. what more can i do because nothing seems to be enough for the gifts i've received. i ask the question, but i'll continue to move until i'm not told anymore, because there's always more. asé/namaste/as above, so below.

—

The "and then what" question doesn't exist

There will never be enough.

When you think about your purpose, what you're meant to do, "how far the rabbit hole goes", there are the questions of "will it ever be enough?" And the answer is no, it won't. The most powerful leaders of the world still have moments of "Am I doing enough?" The divide comes when you allow not being enough to engulf you in the darker areas. Knowing enough is never enough shown with a negative is greed, selfishness, narcissism, god complex, and mania.

But knowing enough is never enough in a positive light, is altruism, compassion, charity, generosity, and gratitude.

The fear of never being great or reaching full potential shouldn't be a fearful concept. As humans, or even as spiritual beings, our magic our power, or abilities, stretch farther than one could actually imagine. We cannot see the depths of our possibilities if we've never deep dived into them. However, once you do, once you get the ball rolling in whatever direction you may, you don't stop. you continue to go, move forward, be greater.

absolute power corrupts absolutely is a false mantra because it leaves out the possibility and consideration of those who aim to use their power in an external sense. absolute power corrupts when that power is internalized, and seeps into areas of ourselves (that we all have the ability to become) where

your body is a temporary apartment

Taking care of your body because you're basically renting it.
Your spirit is a part of high consciousness, a link in the connectivity of spirits. You are more than the physical body, you're existing within it, but it is not yours
Think of it like your first apartment, find pride within it, take care of it, make it as comfortable as possible during your stay. You can be as extreme or lax as you like, it's yours in a sense that it'll be home during your years here.
Treat it as if you want your social security deposit back, knowing you did your best and you deserve it back. You didn't leave holes in the walls, weird stains in the carpet, or garbage everywhere.
For some it's not a first apartment, maybe it's your second, third, fourth, shit it might be your first house (congrats!) your past lives is another story.
Consider when you move into your next temporary home, how would you like it to be given to you?

First and foremost, did you save enough in your first apartment to afford something bigger and better? Can you live up to the standards in your apartment to possibly afford a house next time round? Maybe, maybe not..
But how is it presented to you? What does it look like when you move in? How would you feel if you found out that your new home for the next 60–70 years (gods willing) was infested and infected with a number of (let's say) rodents and insects? Your new home has, mental and physical health defects. Your home's last tenant (oh yes, reincarnation) left you with a huge mess to clean because you (your spirit Self) couldn't afford to find a better space to be housed in.
When putting consciousness in connection to your physical body in this context, it made it easier for me to want to fix this current physical self. I've been in limbo with doing much to it cosmetically for the benefit of others or even, simply laziness, but I realize the cosmetics are not important to me. Sure, I'll decorate this body with comfortable clothing, tattoos and piercings, hair colors, and all the like. But the actual foundation is what I care about.
Is my health where I want it to be?
Am I in control of my emotions?
Does my love overflow into others the way I hope to be overflowed into?

What does my silence sound like?
What does my noise say?
Have I made peace with my painbodies?
Have I prepared myself mentally, emotionally, physically, spiritually, consciously for something bigger and better?
These are all the questions I'm facing as a lifestyle, to be faced over time so when it's time for me to move (ascend to Higher), I know all the answers.

www.ingramcontent.com/pod-product-compliance
Lightning Source LLC
Chambersburg PA
CBHW051754130826
49812CB00033B/1144
9789357215589